SKATE FOR YOUR LIFE

LEO BAKER

PENGUIN WORKSHOP

This book is dedicated to those who came before me—those who made it possible to be myself—LB

PENGUIN WORKSHOP
An Imprint of Penguin Random House LLC, New York

Text copyright © 2021 by Leo Baker. Illustrations copyright © 2021 by Penguin Random House LLC. All rights reserved. Published by Penguin Workshop, an imprint of Penguin Random House LLC, New York. PENGUIN and PENGUIN WORKSHOP are trademarks of Penguin Books Ltd, and the W colophon is a registered trademark of Penguin Random House LLC. Manufactured in China.

Visit us online at www.penguinrandomhouse.com.

Library of Congress Cataloging-in-Publication Data is available upon request.

ISBN 9780593223475   10 9 8 7 6 5 4 3 2 1

PROLOGUE

"Are you a boy or a girl?" Oh. *That* question. The eternal question of my life—the question that seems to follow me everywhere I go.

I can think back to a time when I was out skating with my childhood best friend, Evan, in Covina Park, California. He was two years older than me and had dirty-blond shaggy hair and blue eyes. People always thought we were siblings, and, in a way, it felt like we were. While we'd skate, there was always a group of boys skating in the park with us. One time they confronted me with that question. Evan stood up for me. He told them I was a girl. "So you're a tomboy?" they asked, their faces scrunched up with uncertainty. I shrugged it off and nodded yes, feeling exposed.

Those moments came often, and the truth was that I wanted to say I was a boy. If I had to opt for being either a girl or a boy, the answer was obvious. It was so simple.

I wish I could still say that now. I wish it was really *that* simple. As I've gotten older, the question carries more and more weight. Because to me, the question isn't whether I am a boy or a girl, but rather: Why are there only two options to choose from to begin with?

As a transmasculine person, I notice the look of confusion on people's faces when I speak. My voice sounds feminine to them, so when possible, I opt for not speaking at all. I wear hats and hoods to avoid eye contact with strangers, and I bind my chest to appear flat. Baggy sweatshirts are my best friends. I feel alien in most public spaces, unless of course, it's a queer space. I am hypervigilant in every place I enter because I experience transphobic microaggressions on a daily basis. The blatant dirty looks. The doubt on people's faces. And then, of course, come the questions and comments: "Are you in the correct bathroom?" "Why do you look like a boy?" "The men's bathroom is over there." "Your food is ready, sir. Oops, I mean ma'am!" It gets tiring after a while. Nobody should have to repeatedly explain their existence.

I've found myself explaining my existence my whole life—even as a professional skateboarder. "What do you do for work?" "I'm a . . . professional skater." Their head tilts to the side. It's the same look I get when people realize that I am not a cisgender guy. Skateboarding thrives on the perception of being progressive. One would think that an industry created by outcasts, creatives, and counterculture simply wouldn't tolerate sexism, homophobia, transphobia, and misogyny. But the reality is far different. For years I was pushed aside because the industry didn't know what to do with me. They didn't know how to accept a tomboy skater. I once received an award titled Skates Like a Dude. I was judged by my looks first, my skill level second.

Skateboarding has a complicated past. On the one hand, you have heroes like Patti McGee, Elissa Steamer, and Cara-Beth Burnside who have carved a path for women in skateboarding. Elissa Steamer and

Alexis Sablone are two of my all-time favorite heroes, and they were the first non-male skateboarders I had ever seen. They are pioneers. The future is slowly getting brighter, but it's clear to me that the skate industry needs to take a look at itself with a critical eye. Cisgender white men run the show in the skateboard world. And as long as this is true, folks that don't fall into that category are stuck waiting for a piece of the pie, while large brands take advantage of their stories and use their creativity for their own benefit. The saddest part of this arrangement is that most of the time, those companies don't even realize they're doing it. In a lot of cases, marginalized communities deal with tokenization and exploitation, and the skateboard industry is no exception.

I have been skateboarding since I was around two or three years old. The moment I started, I knew that I wanted to skate for the rest of my life. It was my favorite thing then and remains sacred to me to this day. I fell in love with it because of the simple fact that there are no rules. Skateboarding is steeped in creative expression. Skate how you want, dress how

8

you want, do what you want. The whole world is your playground. Any average person might pull up to a red or yellow curb and think, "no parking" or "loading zone," but when a skater sees a painted curb, they could spend all day skating it, trying trick after trick in order to conquer it. Every day is a new adventure when you are skating. Every day is an opportunity for progress, something new to learn.

My skate career started around age ten when I got my first sponsor, and I have been skateboarding professionally since 2014. I learned the hard way that skateboarding itself is very different from the industry that accompanies it, and moving through this world as a queer, gender nonconforming person has not been an easy feat by any means. But my one hope through it all is that there's a way to create a space for many generations of skateboarding queers to come. That's a mission I can really stand behind. I am extremely grateful for the platform I have and I want to use it to create some kind of change, even if it's only a little bit. I am living a life that I love and opening people's minds by being exactly who I am.

And when I stand for myself, I stand for everyone out there who is as authentically unique as I am. Because my authenticity has never been a burden. It is my superpower.

SKATE FOR YOUR LIFE

Skateboarding and the culture that surrounds it form a giant ball of contradictions. In the 1950s, surfers in California wanted to find a way to surf when the waves were flat, and as a result, skateboarding was born. Quickly, it became a counterculture darling— a symbol of rebellion, freedom, and lawlessness. In fact, a music genre known as skate-punk emerged in California in the late 1970s due to its shared antiestablishment views with the sport. People caught on to the influence that skateboarding had on popular culture, and over time, it infiltrated every part of our ecosystem. It's become the fabric of our fashion, music, television, and art. Major celebrities co-opt core skate brands like *Thrasher* and Supreme, and streetwear is highly informed by skate styles.

When you take something like skateboarding—something so unique and creative—and try to mold it into something as traditional as sports and competition, the results are, well, boring. The roots of skateboarding grew from people who didn't fit in. Creatives, artists, outcasts, kids from broken homes, and loners all found their solace in skateboarding. The culture of skateboarding is beautiful and was a fundamental vehicle for my self-expression. A large part of skateboarding is problem-solving and making something out of nothing. There are no teams, no rules, just you and your skateboard. I discovered that with determination and commitment, the possibilities are endless.

The contest world, by contrast, is not as exciting. There is a formula to competitive skateboarding, so people tend to catch on pretty quickly. Judges reward the skaters for style and when they do big tricks, but there's still a formula to it all. Consistency is major when it comes to competitions, and at the end of the day, a trick down a long rail usually always takes the cake. As a result, the skaters put a lot of their focus on skating rails, getting basic tricks locked in and consistent. I applaud the dedication, but I don't find it that exciting to watch. Especially when everyone is doing the same thing. In a contest, it's amazing to see people try riskier tricks, one's they're not guaranteed to land every time. But even I succumb to the contest formula, and I'm just really bored of it.

Sport and competition are inherently traditional, but then again, so is the construct of gender. And the two are indelibly linked. Traditional sports have strict rules and requirements, and while they encourage teamwork and social interaction, everyone still has to once again answer the question: "Are you a boy or are you a girl?" They're then split into two groups, and more assumptions are made. "Boys are stronger while girls are weaker." "Boys play harder while girls should be lucky they even get to play at all." "Feminine strength isn't as interesting to watch as masculine strength." Add folks who don't fit into the traditional mold of the gender binary into the mix, and the system goes berserk. What's the point in playing at all if we've been playing in a world that wasn't designed to include us?

When you take a person like me, neither fully male nor female, and then put me into the category of "women's skateboarding," I get deprived of everything that makes me who I am. This is the place where I'm robbed of my creativity, my identity, my self-expression, and my humanity. As a queer skateboarder, the competition world just isn't made for me. And due to my gender ambiguity, I also don't truly feel welcome in women's spaces. Constantly hearing the announcers say things like "check out these ladies out on the course!" makes my skin crawl. Very often I am in a space where people don't use my correct pronouns, and I hear my deadname constantly. When they announce my deadname to introduce me for my run and use she/her pronouns, I really just feel invisible. Pronouns feel either really safe or really triggering. When someone gets my pronouns right, it feels good—I feel seen; I feel safe. But when someone gets my pronouns wrong, it feels as if someone is getting my name wrong over and over. That inherently feels like I don't matter. Regardless of who you are, anyone could relate to this.

After I came out as nonbinary, I got comments like these: "Why are you in a woman's contest if you aren't a woman?" "You identify as a woman when there's money involved." "Sell out." "She/her." "You'll always be a female no matter what your name is." "How do you compete in women's events your whole career but now you're a dude? Stop being a weirdo hipster." Comments like these break me down, but I do my best to ignore them. I realize that I could engage with these folks, but my mental health is more important to me than proving a point. It would ultimately be another experience of me trying to explain my existence. If I could wave a magic wand and have everyone in the world be willing to understand the trans experience, I'd do that. But the fact of the matter is that these issues are too complex to resolve with internet trolls who have little interest in learning about my experience, anyway.

People in the skate industry have known me as

"Lacey Baker" since the beginning. It feels impossible to break away from that. The more I grow into who I am as a trans/gender nonconforming person, the more I feel its effects when people misgender me. Whenever I find myself in a situation where I am unable to fully express myself, my physical experience shifts majorly. Depression and anxiety manifest themselves in everything I do. My instinct is to isolate. It kills my motivation to do anything. Being in survival mode is worlds away from actually living.

I discovered skating around the time I could walk, and have been enthralled with it ever since. When I was about two or three years old, my sister, April, and I were in foster care for a short period of time in La Verne, California. I had two teenage foster brothers, Matt and Zach. I really looked up to them and wanted to be just like them. If they played baseball in the yard, I wanted to play with them. If they threw a football, I wanted to catch it. I felt safe with them. At the time, they had a skate ramp in the backyard. I watched them skate all day, gazing up at them as they dropped in, pumping back and forth, taking turns. The ramp was huge, maybe as big as a fourteen-foot half-pipe. Or maybe, now that I think about it, I was just really, really small. But I wasn't afraid of it—I was enamored. I wanted to get up there.

It wasn't long before I got a skateboard of my own. In the car one day, my foster mom asked me what I wanted for Easter, and without hesitation, I exclaimed that I wanted a skateboard. She was skeptical. I think she was surprised that a young girl would be interested in skating. "Are you sure?" she asked, looking concerned. I insisted, and we went to buy my first board. I had never experienced such a rush of joy and excitement before—and then I saw it: a board that had a cartoon drawing of a blue bulldog chained up to a red doghouse. He was scary looking and fierce. I thought it looked so cool and I wanted to be cool. I knew it was the one, and when we finally got back to the house, I rushed to the backyard with the board under my arm.

Something about getting to pick my own board was special. It's a recurring theme in skateboarding. Your board is an extension of your self-expression. It's a piece of you. Something about that board spoke to me, so having it was maybe one of my first experiences of independence. I tried to copy exactly what Matt and Zach did on the board. I didn't know any trick names, but I watched how they would pop the board and jump in the air, so I attempted to do the same over and over. I later learned that this trick is called an ollie. I can remember being outside one dewy morning, standing at the bottom of the ramp just trying to nudge back and forth.

A year or two later, my birth mom regained custody of April and me, and we moved back into my grandma's house in Covina. It wasn't an easy household to live in. My grandma was strict and played favorites. It was a tense environment. She wasn't always nice to me and she was never nice to April. For some reason she only really showed love to my older brother Chris, who lived with her before we moved back in. He never even had to go to foster care. Our grandma refused to care for April and me when our mom was putting her life back together. To this day I still don't understand why she treated us the way she did. When I was in elementary school, my grandma would often force me to wear skirts and shoes with heels. I hated when she did that, especially because heels made it harder to play sports during recess. In the moments when my Grandma would make me dress feminine, my mom was either at work or school. So I had no choice but to accept it.

With my mom, it was a different story. When I was with her, I was safe to wear and do whatever I wanted. She would let me wear Chris's clothes and would always let me pick out the shoes I wanted. We would go through the McDonald's drive-thru and if there was a choice, she would choose the boy toy for me. I never had to explain. She just knew me like that.

When we reunited, my mom dedicated herself to staying sober, starting a career, and making sure that she never lost us to the foster care system again. But because my grandma wasn't willing to look after us, my mom was almost always forced to take my sister and me everywhere, including Narcotics Anonymous meetings. It was good news for me, though, because the Saturday meetings were held in Covina Park and that meant I was able to skate.

One Saturday night, April, my mom, and I were

getting ready to go to a meeting together. I was maybe seven years old; my sister was eight. I was wearing Chris's baggy blue jean shorts that went way past my knees and his white Gap T-shirt, which was so big, I could practically swim in it. But truth be told, I felt amazing. I was excited to go skate in the park and I felt safe because my grandma wouldn't be there to scold me for dressing like a boy. I felt like me.

As I was getting ready in the bathroom, I looked in the mirror and began to notice my long blond hair. The dead giveaway—the one thing that didn't feel like me. *People probably wouldn't even know I'm a girl if it wasn't for this stupid hair*, I thought to myself. I always felt like I passed for a boy pretty well, except for when my grandma would make me wear my hair down. This time I wanted to try something new. I pulled my hair back as tight as I could. I put it into a ponytail and tucked it into my brother's brown and black suede cap with the words *Top Gun* embroidered across the front of it. That was the first time I felt like I didn't have to compromise myself so that the world would accept me.

That evening, my mom, my sister, and I arrived at the meeting in Covina Park. The park was tucked away in the suburbs right near Downtown Covina, surrounded by ordinary rows of houses and a hospital across the street. There was an outdoor auditorium in the middle of the park, a jungle gym, a track, an outdoor roller rink, and a long stretch of field. The meeting was set up in the field. While my mom listened and shared stories, April and I were free to run around and play in the park. There were only two conditions: 1. Stay in the park and 2. Do not talk to strangers.

I had my skateboard under my arm as April and I walked to the playground. A little boy about our age came up to play with us. As we were playing, he looked me up and down and then asked, "Are you a boy or a girl?" I knew I was suited up enough to claim that I was a boy, and that's what I told him. But my sister was confused. She gave me a look and immediately said I was a girl. I insisted that I was a boy and managed to hide my frustration, but I was outed. I tried so hard to figure out ways to get away with it. I felt like I had no choice but to "be a girl."

After that night in the park, a lot of my time was spent trying to pass, or appear, as a boy. I'd find myself in the bathroom, door locked, obsessing over my hair. I'd slick it back into a tight ponytail and look at myself from different angles, trying to see a boy in the reflection. *Maybe,* I thought, *if I concentrate hard enough I'll just magically turn into one.* The bathroom was a small but safe place for me to explore my gender. I could dress myself as a boy and not really have to deal with the outside world asking me who I was or trying to make me into something I wasn't. The feeling of seeing a reflection in the mirror that didn't feel like me was, in a word, exhausting. For most of my life, I didn't know that what I was experiencing has a name—gender dysphoria. And just like the question "Are you a boy or a girl" has followed me down every path of my life, so has dysphoria. The only thing that saved me was skateboarding.

☆   ☆   ☆

Skateboarding gave me a place to focus my energy in ways I felt I had more control over. It's all I cared about. Every weekend, when I was around nine and ten years old, I would spend the night at my best friend Evan's house. Usually, we would meet up at Saturday night's NA meeting, since his parents were also in the program, and the adventures would commence. We would always start at the auditorium in the park, repeatedly doing ollies and one-eighties down a five-stair set. If we got bored, we could skate in any direction and just find new spots. We would find gaps, stairs, and waxed curbs. As long as we were back by the end of the meeting, we could go anywhere we wanted.

The sleepovers were the best. Evan introduced me to so much in those years. We watched skate videos, made mixed CDs, played *Tony Hawk's Pro Skater*, and ate junk food. The morning routine was to eat cereal and watch cartoons before skating around the neighborhood all day long. He would always let me wear his clothes, too, which I loved. We skated off stages and through the halls in local schools, or found loading docks behind our local grocery stores. There were moments when I had no idea where we were, but I always knew Evan would stick by my side.

One day we started off in Azusa, a small neighboring town of Covina, and ended up in Industry City because Evan wanted to ollie this nine-stair set over a sidewalk into the parking lot. We found a loading dock on the way. "I want to just one-eighty it really quick!" I said. "Go for it!" he replied encouragingly. I got up there and went for it but I was a little overconfident. All I can remember was coming down off the four-foot drop and feeling my chin get knocked by my board. "Are you okay?" "Yeah, I think so . . ." I was in a daze. My chin was dripping blood, and Evan helped me clean it off. I was trying to collect myself because I wanted to keep skating, but as we rolled through the parking lot, I saw more blood dripping out of my chin onto my board. I definitely needed stitches but was too afraid to tell anyone. I knew my mom couldn't afford it and I didn't want to stress her out. Eventually, the bleeding stopped, and we skated for the rest of the day, as usual. When we got back to Evan's after the sun went down, we scoured the medicine cabinet and found these Band-Aids that somehow blended in with my skin perfectly, and nobody ever had to know that I needed stitches. It was our secret—and it was safe.

My obsession with skating and everything that came with it only deepened as the years went on. Back in fourth grade, there was this pair of skate shoes I really wanted. It was a pair of Etnies, specifically—the Mike Vallely pro model. They were bulky, which was the trend for skate shoes back then. These ones were all black with a rubber toe cap and a mix of mesh and suede along the side panels. The tongue was puffy, complete with the Etnies logo at the top. Mike Vallely put lightning bolts on all his pro boards and merchandise (he has two giant lightning bolt tattoos on his forearms), so of course the shoes had a white outline of a lightning bolt on the back. A kid in my school had them; he was a fifth grader, and I wanted those shoes so bad, I begged my mom to get them for me. She took me to Utility Board Shop in Covina to get me those shoes, but they didn't have my size.

Christmastime came around, and there was a huge box for me under the tree. I couldn't even begin to guess what was inside. The anticipation grew as Christmas morning approached. Money was usually pretty tight, but my mom always did her best to get us a couple of gifts each. That year the only thing under the tree for me was that huge box. It was there for weeks; so when Christmas morning came, I ripped into it as fast as I could, only to find a lot of crumpled tissue paper and newspaper. And then more tissue paper. (And then more.) I was so confused. I felt like I was digging into a black hole. I looked up at my mom like, *What?* She gestured for me to keep looking. Finally, as I reached the bottom of the box, there they were: the Mike Vallely pro model Etnies! I put the shoes on immediately, and I don't think I took them off until I completely shredded them to pieces.

There was one more present for me. Because they

didn't have my size at the Covina shop, my mom had to go to the Utility Board Shop in La Verne, just a few towns east of Covina. At the checkout counter, she saw a stack of flyers for skateboarding classes that started in the spring. In addition to the shoes, my mom enrolled me in the skate classes. The instructor's name was Ryan Miller. Little did my mom know that she would introduce me to someone who would change my life forever.

For the month of March, I got to see Ryan for an hour a week on Sundays, and he taught me whatever I wanted to learn. He would assess what I could do and then give me the tools to build off the skills I already had. Ryan was raised in the Inland Empire in Southern California. He grew up skating through the nineties and he was twenty-four when we met. Ryan was in school to become a teacher and his side hustle was skate classes. My mom would drop me off with Ryan at the park and we—along with three other young boys—would skate flat ground on the basketball court for an hour. After the first session, Ryan told my mom that I was too advanced for the beginner class, but she asked if I could complete it anyways. When the four sessions were over, my mom asked if Ryan would be interested in mentoring me privately. Ryan immediately agreed. After the lessons went private, I got to practice in the skate park. I had a pretty good foundation to work from, and Ryan really showed me that the possibilities were endless—that the way you can conquer the ground is done with simple, calculated adjustments: the way your foot is positioned on the board, or the way your body curves and leans, or even the confidence and curiosity with which you go into trying a new trick. Most importantly, he taught me that there's no right way to skate. That possibilities and complications should be welcomed and embraced.

Eventually, Ryan told my mom that she didn't have to pay him anymore, and he just started picking me up to go skate. By the time summer rolled around, a strong foundation of trust had developed between him and my mom, so he was able to take me skating anywhere. We skated many spots, but one of my favorite days ever was the first time he took me to skate at Chaffey High School with all his friends. Chaffey High is a legendary skate spot in the Inland Empire. Rolling up to the spot, my mind went blank and I just thought, *Oh my god skate heaven*. I felt like I was in some sacred skateboarding land. There were ledges as far as the eye could see, each one blackened from years of being waxed and skated. Most of the ledges were above my knees, all rounded and chunky from countless grinds over the years—I'd never skated a spot like this before. I was only ten years old, skating with a group of guys in their early twenties, and even though I was intimidated, witnessing their camaraderie was so special. It felt good to see friends encouraging one another to keep pushing. Some were filming each other doing new tricks while others were playing SKATE or just trying to learn new stuff. The sounds of trucks grinding across the concrete ledges and the clicks of the wheels going over the cracks were all so magical.

"This is where I learned how to skate. There were no skate parks when I was growing up," Ryan said as we left Chaffey that evening. It blew me away.

I learned so much from skating with Ryan. Despite the age difference, we were two people who just really loved skating, and he had so much to share. He exposed me to so much about skateboarding's history and let me borrow his nineties skate VHS tapes and his paint markers to draw on my grip tape. My mind was on overdrive—and I wondered how I could fit into all of this. This world that felt so vast and rich. The truth was, I definitely had my work cut out for me.

Ryan's generosity impacted me even more that same year when he vouched for me to get my first sponsorship with Utility Board Shop in La Verne. The deal was that I'd get one board a month plus a shirt, a hat, and shop stickers. It all happened so fast. I met Ryan in the spring and was sponsored by summer. I felt like I was really *doing it*. Like, on my way to becoming a pro skater. I was determined, and with Ryan and Utility Board Shop behind me, I was lit up like never before. It felt so good to be seen. I called Evan as my mom and I left the shop the day that I got my sponsorship, telling him about all the free stuff I'd get every month. Evan was happy for me; so was my mom. I clutched the stack of Utility Board Shop stickers in my hand all the way home, flipping through them and admiring all the colors and the plasticky smell, thinking of all the things I'd sticker up. It was a huge deal for me. My dreams were coming true.

Through family and friends, I also started to get introduced to other sponsors, like Billabong, and shortly after signing with them, Ryan recommended that I start competing in California Amateur Skateboard League (CASL). CASL holds a series of competitions once a month at different skate parks in Southern California. Since there were no other girl skaters in the league, I was competing against boys in my age bracket. In all the years I spent competing in CASL, I think I got only two trophies. "Just have fun. It's not about winning. It's about the experience," my mom would say to me. So I kept pushing.

I competed in my first women's contest just a few days before my thirteenth birthday. My mom was worried they wouldn't let me skate because all the contestants had to be thirteen or older to participate, but she took me anyway. This was the moment I met some of the best women skateboarders on the planet. Before that point, I thought that Elissa Steamer was the only non-male skater besides me. That's why I was so blown away when I met everyone—legends like Jaime Reyes, Vanessa Torres, and Lisa Whitaker. These people paved the way for future generations, including me. Jaime Reyes was one of only two women skaters ever to get the cover of *Thrasher* magazine, in April of 1994. Vanessa Torres was pro for Element, and has style so flawless, she's still one of my favorite skaters to this day. Lisa Whitaker has made a huge impact on the progress of women's skateboarding. She is responsible for the first decade of women's skate footage. She dedicated herself to filming women skaters when nobody else would and single-handedly created platforms for visibility of women who skate. She filmed and edited the first all-women's skate documentary, *Getting Nowhere Faster*, and went on to create thesideproject.com, which later evolved into girlsskatenetwork.com, to further the progress and visibility that much more. Not to mention the fact that she created a board company called Meow Skateboards to support us during a time when barely any companies would. I didn't realize just how powerful it was to be in a space with all of these incredible humans.

The competition was jam format. The skaters get separated into heats, and each heat gets five minutes all together on the course. When you land a trick you get points, and if you miss a trick it doesn't count against you. This takes the pressure off in comparison to run format, where missing a trick does count against you. The prize was a free trip to Australia to compete in a World Cup Skateboarding competition called the Global Assault. I wondered if it was possible. If I could really have a chance at winning. I could hear my mom's voice ringing, "Just do your best! It's not about winning, it's about having fun." And that's exactly what I did. A big part of me wanted to prove myself, but I was grateful no matter what.

I can't remember much of the contest, but I do remember the focus I had. I did my best to land everything: all the tricks I'd practiced over and over, all the hours and days and months spent practicing until my consistency was close to flawless. This was my moment to show that. Toward the end of the jam, I got up on a four-foot ledge and started trying a frontside flip off of it. I knew I could do it because of all those days skating loading docks with Evan. I just thought of it as the same thing. I landed it and right there, I won my first contest. Everyone was so excited for me, especially my mom. She rushed through the people, glowing with pride, arms wide open ready to wrap me up in a big squeeze. She couldn't stop smiling. She squeezed my face and laughed as I stood there in awe of what had just happened. All of a sudden, I was holding a giant boarding pass to fly to the other side of the world. I'd never even been on a plane before and had no idea what to expect. But I was in shock, realizing I'd be flying for fifteen hours to compete in the Global Assault. I'd shown the skate world what I was capable of, and it paid off. I was going to Australia.

Still buzzing on the way home, I felt like I was shining with excitement. All the tension left my body and I was slowly taking it all in. "It doesn't matter what happens in Australia," my mom said. "It doesn't matter if you fall on your butt through the whole contest. It's all about right now, this feeling. Today is what you've been working so hard for." She didn't want me to get bigheaded about winning, and she never wanted to see me disappointed. I've always held this close to the chest. It has kept my heart full and my feet on the ground.

I knew nothing about World Cup Skateboarding, but that moment was my induction into that world. Everything was so surreal. Exploring Australia with my newfound friends was unforgettable. I bonded with so many amazing people and I had so much fun practicing for the contest. The jet lag had me exhausted; the whole thing felt like a dream, so I just took it a little at a time. I finished fourth place, and that felt perfectly okay. No disappointment at all— I just had a sense of ease and peacefulness to have had such an amazing opportunity.

After the Global Assault, I was a regular contender in World Cup Skateboarding contests, and traveling became the norm. I saw so many beautiful places at such a young age. I was just wide-eyed and curious. Companies also began to see my potential, and I started to get more sponsors. Through the years, those sponsors put more and more emphasis on my marketability as a "female skater." Especially Billabong. But with them being the ones to fly me to all the contests, I felt backed into a corner. The more I gave in, the more praise I got. People always commented on my long blond hair. Suddenly, the one thing I wanted to get rid of happened to be the ticket to my dreams.

The more I conformed, the more success I gained. I was slowly drifting further and further away from who I was. It happened over the course of a few years in little ways. First, it was, "Just get this one pair of girl jeans to try out!" So I did. and then it was, "The higher-ups here at Billabong really need you to be in the girls stuff because you are technically on the girl's program." No more baggy pants, no more big shirts. I felt like the only thing they let me keep was a backward hat. I'd been molded into their little

41

dream skater girl. I did my best to make the clothes feel somewhat me. After a while of feeling ridiculous in flared jeans, I learned how to taper the bottoms. April showed me that I could sew up the inseams of my pants with dental floss, because the thread I was using wouldn't hold up during skate sessions. I'd tie the backs of the tank tops so the front covered more of my chest. I was becoming "Lacey Baker" in front of everyone's eyes, but that wasn't really *me*. I was so caught up in what people wanted me to be that I lost touch with myself without even noticing. But as long as I was skating, I was more or less happy.

I had felt so much confidence as a child, looking in the mirror in all my brother's clothes, standing in my truth. But by this point, when I looked in the mirror it all seemed so false. The clothes I wore were really getting to me. It was always a compromise. I'd get the clothes from Billabong and try to alter them to make them work for me. But they were always so bad. It was like solving a puzzle. "How can I make these ill-fitting ugly pants a *little* better?" The truth was that I hated those clothes. A pull here, a push there, a broken stitch, the crotch of my pants blowing out, constantly tugging my shirt down, buttons popping off, my underwear and butt crack hanging out because the pants were cut too low, and to top that off, I was always trying to get my hair out of my eyes. Was it really *that* marketable? Really?

Clothing is a huge mode of self-expression for me as a skater and as a queer person. The importance of feeling at home in one's body is a universal truth. By compromising my presentation, I was compromising my identity. It was all so hollow. I didn't even get a chance to find my identity before one was created for me. The whole thing was phony, so at seventeen I began shopping for clothes that I actually wanted, even though I'd get clothes for free. The compromise was over. Under contract I was required to wear a logo during competitions, so I'd do that. But any other time it was all about black jeans and a plain white shirt. I was rediscovering a part of myself that I forgot was there all along. I was slowly peeling back the layers, like papier-mâché in reverse. There was so much to discover. It's a long process to remove the parts of ourselves we create to survive. It felt good to do what I wanted, but that liberation came with a price.

My self-expression cost me. The skate industry didn't want a butchy, queer skater; they only had eyes for the "pretty" femmes, especially after the recession in 2008. Companies began cutting skaters, and budgets thinned out. Billabong discarded their skate program entirely, so that was the end of that, and Element let me go, too. "You haven't been doing enough," they told me. "We aren't going to renew your contract."

I wasn't expecting that. I thought I was doing great, considering I was in *Thrasher* magazine just months before, doing well in contests, and filming in the streets consistently. I was caught off guard. I'd been so loyal to that brand, but things were changing fast. "You can still get free boards whenever you want, but you'll have to earn your contract back." I think it was just an excuse to get rid of me, because at the same time, they brought in new amateurs and kept all the pros. And when I reached out to get boards, they just brushed me off to the next person, then the next, until I just stopped asking. I felt like I was grasping at straws for support, especially from a company where I once felt at home, but it became clear really quickly that there was nothing left.

My skate career almost came to a full stop. It was disheartening to see, when other more feminine skaters still had everything. People just didn't know what to do with me. It made me feel othered and pushed aside. I was so dedicated to skateboarding that I couldn't really comprehend the reality of the situation: After all those years of hard work, there was just, nothing. Apart from Pawnshop Skate Co. and Lisa Whitaker helping me out, there wasn't much else going on. Pawnshop was my new local shop sponsor, since Utility had gone out of business a while back. I still had competitions to look forward to, but during that time they were sparse—one, maybe two a year. The World Cup Skateboarding contests were still happening, but I didn't have the funds to get there.

A big problem was that I hadn't yet understood the difference between skateboarding itself and capital *S* Skateboarding, the business. That my love for skating should have never been measured by the approval of the industry. I didn't know it at the time, but this hugely impacted my skating. I struggled to enjoy it. I thought people had my back, but in reality, all they wanted was an image. I no longer fit that image, so they no longer cared. I know that skateboarding never owed me anything, but I felt like I earned a spot somewhere on the roster. And for the first time ever, I actually thought it was all going to end.

I always knew I wouldn't be able to skate forever. Skateboarding is harder on the body in comparison to traditional sports. Landing on concrete over and over wears you down pretty fast, so a skateboarding career can last only so long. Injuries aren't a matter of if, they're a matter of when. In some cases you can ride your professional skate career out well into your sixties, but not without other ties in the industry. You either start your own skate company, work in the industry, or you're Tony Hawk. Either way, I knew I needed a fallback plan for my future—I just didn't think that time would come when I was nineteen.

Straight out of high school, I went to the Art Institute of California, and I worked toward a bachelor's degree in graphic design. Graphic design seemed like a good fit because I was always into painting and drawing. I've always loved working with my hands and being creative. Graphic design seemed to go hand in hand with skateboarding also, and I always wanted to do my own board graphics. It was the perfect exit strategy. Going to school as a fallback plan saved me. My career in skating left me with no choice but to graduate with an associate's degree instead of a bachelor's, but I was lucky regardless. After I graduated, I got hired in the marketing department at a lighting company called Luminance, in Commerce, California. I was fortunate enough to be able to find a job, and even more fortunate that it was a job I liked.

It was the right move for me. I absolutely loved my boss and my team. We had fun working together. And the best part? It had *nothing* to do with skateboarding. Working a graphic design job at a lighting company was worlds away from all of that. It felt good to close that door. I was able to be creative, and it was a much-needed escape from a world where I felt like

I didn't belong. I continued to skate for fun—that was something I never wanted to give up—but I no longer had to sacrifice any parts of myself for anyone. No sponsors breathing down my neck, nobody telling me how they think I should look, I felt valued and appreciated at my job, which was truly a breath of fresh air, compared to my previous life.

It took me years to realize how powerful of a move that actually was: to stay true to myself, even if that meant giving up on the dream. I needed time to find myself, and after a while, I started to feel sort of okay again. I finally had stability, and of course, I had my skateboard. X Games still had a women's contest, so I continued to compete there. That was all there was for me. One contest a year. But I had friends who had my back, and I was surviving. I was slowly rebuilding myself and rediscovering my own humanity. I felt like I was coming alive, and it was even more of a reason to skate my heart out again. I stood in my power. I wouldn't budge any longer, and if the skating industry wasn't going to accept me, I was going to have to make it despite them.

Progress on my board was slower, but I felt curious again. What would it be like to reenter the skate world on my own terms? I decided to film a video part with my friend Tyler Smolinski. A video part is footage of all your best skating, and skaters work tirelessly to film their best stuff. It's usually anywhere from two and a half to five minutes long, but the process itself is a drawn-out, agonizing pursuit. Sometimes it takes years to figure out a trick and film. You fall and get back up, and fall and get back up. Sometimes it's frustrating, sometimes it's terrifying, and sometimes you want to give up forever. Sometimes you land a trick only once in your life. Tyler and I toiled on my part for the next two years or so. It took longer than usual because I had a nine-to-five, and I was able to film only on the weekends. Some days we'd meet after I got off work, but rarely was it successful. But the moments when I landed a new trick were the ones that kept me going—not the falls. The sound of my trucks grinding across a concrete ledge, or my wheels clicking over bricks, or the scrape of the tail on a sewer cap. The humming of the wheels when I skated down a long stretch of asphalt, feeling the air on my face. It was magic to me. The world went silent.

After sitting behind a desk for two and a half years, in 2016, I realized that I really needed to focus on skating. I got antsy. My boss could tell I was unhappy, and on a whim, I decided to put in my two-week notice. I didn't even think about it; I just followed my instincts and took the leap. I got a freelance graphic design gig, which gave me a lot more free time to focus on skating and allowed me to travel more freely, too. I went to New York for the first time that summer in 2016, and stayed for the whole month of August. I was absolutely enamored and fell in love instantly. New York gave me life in a way that I had never felt when I was living in Los Angeles. Tyler came for a weekend that month and we finished up the filming for my video part. We skated all day long, all over the city. It felt good to be on the ground and in the subway. The traffic in Los Angeles can make street skating a challenge. Something about sitting in a car for hours and then trying to warm up and film a trick is just hard for me. In New York, the momentum is electrifying and instant. Every day feels like a day well spent, and it doesn't take too much planning to make stuff happen. I felt like I was rediscovering skateboarding in a way I never had before.

Tyler and I worked so hard filming this part, just the two of us. We had no financial backing from any kind of sponsors, which isn't typical for a pro skater. We did all we could with what we had. Once we finally finished it, the part was set to go live on *Thrasher*'s website in January 2017. We called it *My World*. I felt a sense of redemption when it went live, like maybe this time things could be different. I couldn't wait for the world to see it. I wanted to show my dedication to skating, and Tyler captured it all perfectly. Best of all, it was all clips of *me*, skating as *me*, with nobody telling *me* how to be.

I was fired up again. I booked a flight back to Los Angeles in early September to compete in the Street League Skateboarding (SLS) Super Crown World Championships. If it wasn't for that, I maybe never would have left New York. Going into that contest, I really felt like I had nothing to lose. The women's side of skateboarding is very tight-knit, and we all joked about how patronizing it was to have such a large pay discrepancy. The men's first place prize was $200K, a shockingly high number compared to $30K for women's first place. But it was an opportunity to win some cash nonetheless, and I knew if I won, it would be possible to move to New York.

The contest day came fast. I felt really good about how I'd been skating in practice. I was nervous; the minutes felt like hours. It felt like everything was on the line and, at the same time, like nothing mattered at all. I really wanted it this time. Competitions don't mean much to me because the essence of skating to me is not about winning. I skate to have fun. But there was something looming over me this time, a drive that made me feel like I had something to prove. The arena was packed with fans roaring and yelling, but I couldn't hear any of them. Everything was silent for me. It was just me and my skateboard, just like it's always been.

The format at SLS consists of two forty-five second runs, followed by a best trick section. Here is where

54

you have an opportunity to really prove yourself. You get five chances to land tricks on any obstacle of your choice, and the scores show on the Jumbotron in real time. Scores range from one to ten and add up accordingly, with your two lowest scores getting dropped to get your final count.

The contest began. There were ten of us competing, and my name was at the bottom of the roster. I always prefer to go first because it just feels better to get it over with. But I stood there waiting for my turn. It felt like a lifetime. I paced back and forth in my starting spot to keep myself in the zone. I remained focused on deep breathing, never paying attention to anyone else's runs. I wasn't going to let anything psych me out. They finally called my name and I took my first run. Everything fell silent, again—a complete blur. I was so concentrated on my run that only after it ended did I realize that I landed everything. One tiny moment of relief came over me before I had to go back to my starting point and do it all over again, waiting, pacing, breathing. I tried to keep my poise, too, because I knew there were hundreds of people watching, not only in the arena, but all over the world.

They called my name again, and I took my second run. Silence. Blurriness. Adrenaline. I landed everything again. Time flew by, and before I knew it, I was circulating around first place. But it wasn't over yet—I also knew that Leticia Bufoni had a plan to do a trick that would have put her into first place. She wanted to do a massive gap into a lipslide on the rail, which would gain her major points. Leticia and I have known each other for over a decade; we used to go street skating with Lisa all the time when we were teens. She's extremely talented. She attempted the trick, but she slammed, hard. She got carried out on a stretcher. It was awful to witness. But that was it. I took my last run and I won my first SLS Super Crown Championship. I was on a cloud. All my closest friends were there hugging me, proud and happy yells filling the air in every direction. My sister was there, and so was my mom. She had the same smile on her face that she did when I won that first contest when I was twelve. My whole body was buzzing from the adrenaline. The people, the fans, the cameras, my friends, my family, everything—it's so overwhelming. I can admit, even though I don't care too much for competitions, that it feels really good to win.

My World dropped a few months after winning the SLS Super Crown Championship, in 2016. With my chest bound and my head shaved, my authenticity was the foundation of my courage and drive. It was my armor and it was impenetrable. It gave me strength and power to skate my hardest. I knew I stood out from the rest, and I was proud. I wasn't skating for my life anymore. I was skating for myself.

☆   ☆   ☆

In the fall of 2016, shortly after the SLS Super Crown, I moved to New York City. It felt like everything was coming together perfectly. I settled into an apartment in Bed-Stuy, New York, and with the success of *My World* and being the SLS Super Crown Champion, Nike SB offered me a spot on their team. Only this time, I was embraced for exactly who I was. They wanted me because of who I proved myself to be. Because I didn't budge in the face of an industry that was so narrow-minded.

Being in New York also made me feel alive and free in a way that I never felt in Los Angeles. I love being one tiny little person in a city of millions of people, and the more I skated, the more I discovered the communities of skaters all around New York. It was that Chaffey High School feeling all over again. I began to uncover the diversity within the scene— so much beauty, so much camaraderie, so much love. It was inspiring to see so many women and queer folks skating. I didn't feel so alien anymore. I was understood.

Witnessing this amazing community, I wondered how we could push it all further. The work that nonprofit organization Skate Like a Girl was doing out in Seattle inspired me to look into my local community and see how we could come together. I wanted to create a space that felt like home, where women, and queer folk and kids could express themselves freely and without judgment. I felt like New York deserved to have this. So in 2019, I teamed up with Kristin Ebeling, the director of Skate Like a Girl in Seattle, and we set out to create The NYC Skate Project. Having an intentional space where non-cis men could come together and learn how to skate would not only create a stronger foundation for our community within skateboarding, but it would open up the door for anyone of this demographic to begin skating and grow.

We must build the spaces we want to see in the world out of the moments where we do not see ourselves. My dream for The NYC Skate Project is rooted in what I wanted to see when I was growing up—but just didn't. There wasn't a space for women and queer people to have a say and to be creative and explore. That's why The NYC Skate Project belongs to all of us, and we make it whatever we want it to be. A staple of the project includes skateboarding workshops for all ages and abilities, but we've also had live music, art shows, and workshops of all kinds. We do this in the name of celebrating, elevating, and expanding our community. That's where the magic lies. That's real power.

The creation of The NYC Skate Project has given me so much hope. I have seen firsthand how receptive people are to being of service and helping one another with open arms and open hearts. It gives me hope that maybe the future of skateboarding can be inclusive. It gives me hope that there will be equity for marginalized communities, and slowly, as we work to dismantle the systems in place that work against us, that people who skate will become people who skate *with us*.

So, back to that eternal question—are you a boy or a girl?

Does it even matter?

ABOUT US

Pocket Change Collective was born out of a need for space. Space to think. Space to connect. Space to be yourself. And this is your invitation to join us.

These books are small, but they are mighty. They ask big questions and propose even bigger solutions. They show us that no matter where we come from or where we're going, we can all take part in changing the communities around us. Because the possibilities of how we can use our space for good are endless.

So thank you. Thank you for picking this book up. Thank you for reading. Thank you for being a part of the Pocket Change Collective.